Mighty
AIRCRAFT

Ian Graham

FR   TS
LONDON•SYDNEY

An Appleseed Editions book

First published in 2006 by Franklin Watts

Paperback edition 2008

Franklin Watts
338 Euston Road, London NW1 3BH

Franklin Watts Australia
Level 17/207 Kent St, Sydney, NSW 2000

© 2006 Appleseed Editions

Appleseed Editions Ltd
Well House, Friars Hill, Guestling, East Sussex TN35 4ET

Created by Q2A Creative
Editor: Chester Fisher
Designers: Meetu Gupta, Ashita Murgai
Picture Researcher: Deepti Baruah

ISBN 978 0 7496 7587 5

Dewey Classification: 629.133

A CIP catalogue for this book is available from the British Library.

Picture credits
t=top b=bottom c=centre l=left r=right
Airbus: 13t, Anthony Noble: 11b, Benjamin Freer: 19t, Bo Kim: 21b, Bombardier Inc.: 14b, 15t, 15b,
Charlie Mauzé – RotorImage Photos: 22b, Flavien Breitenmoser: 17t, Ian Nightingale: Cover,
Johan Jnijn: 18-19b, Matthew Hom: 10c, Mick Freer: 25t, NASA: 5t, 16b (Above), 16b (Below), 29b,
Northrop Grumman Corporation: 29t, OFFICIAL US Air Force photograph, US Air Force Flight Test Center,
Edwards AFB, CA: 20b, 21t, 24c, 24b, Richard Seaman: 27b, Rolls-Royce plc.: Samuel V. Smith: 27t,
Science And Society Library: 8b (Above), 9b, The Embassy Visual Effects Inc.: 28b,
US Navy photo by Photographer's Mate 3rd Class Andrew King: 23c, Virgin Atlantic: 26c, www.1000aircraftphotos.com:
11t, www.griffwason.com: Library: 8b (Below), www.SamChuiPhotos.com: 6b

Printed in Singapore

Franklin Watts is a division of Hachette Children's Books

CONTENTS

MIGHTY AIRCRAFT

Every year, nearly two billion people take to the air in aircraft. Aircraft take people on holiday, transport goods and defend countries in wartime. It's hard to imagine a world without aircraft.

TYPES OF AIRCRAFT

There are passenger planes, military planes, cargo planes and experimental planes. Passenger planes include small propeller planes, bigger business jets and even bigger airliners. Military planes include fighters, bombers and spy planes. Cargo planes carry freight instead of passengers.

Business jet

Every day, airliners queue up to take off from busy airports.

4

Aircraft are guided on the ground and through the air by air traffic controllers. They talk to the pilots by radio and watch the aircraft movements on their screens.

Airliner

Cargo plane

Fighter

DESIGNING AIRCRAFT

Planes are different shapes and sizes because they are designed to be used in different ways. Fighter planes are small, fast and heavily armed. Cargo planes are bigger, so they can carry lots of cargo. They also have large doors for loading and unloading quickly. Airliners have big cabins for carrying passengers. Business jets are smaller, because they carry fewer people. Robot planes are even smaller because there is no pilot inside.

FAST FACTS
Busiest Airport
The world's busiest airport is Chicago's O'Hare International Airport in the US, with nearly one million take-offs and landings a year.

HOW PLANES FLY

From the smallest single-engine plane to the biggest airliner, all aeroplanes work in much the same way.

UP, UP AND AWAY!

Planes are designed to do three things: their engines propel them through the air, their wings lift them into the sky, and parts of their wings and tail move to steer them. The moving parts are the ailerons in the wings and the elevators and rudder in the tail.

The most important parts of a plane are shown here.

Body
Slim and smooth to move through the air easily

Engines
Propel the plane

Wings
Lift the plane off the ground

Rudder
Swings the tail to the left or right

Elevators
Pitch the nose up or down

Ailerons
Make the plane roll

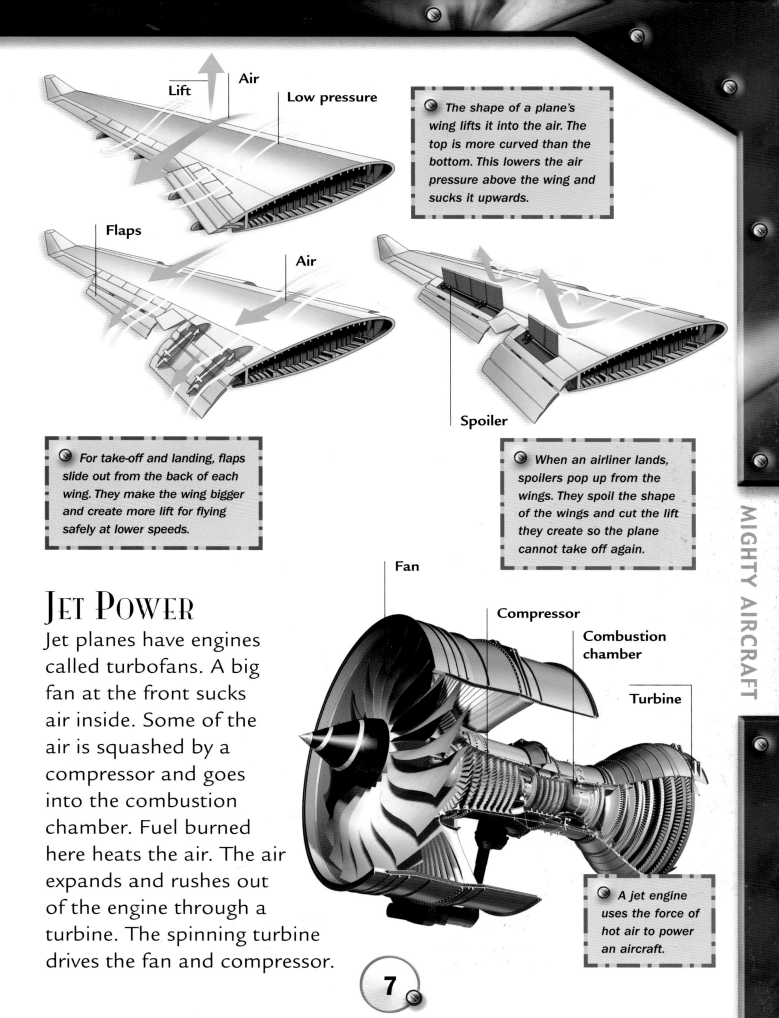

Lift

Air

Low pressure

The shape of a plane's wing lifts it into the air. The top is more curved than the bottom. This lowers the air pressure above the wing and sucks it upwards.

Flaps

Air

Spoiler

For take-off and landing, flaps slide out from the back of each wing. They make the wing bigger and create more lift for flying safely at lower speeds.

When an airliner lands, spoilers pop up from the wings. They spoil the shape of the wings and cut the lift they create so the plane cannot take off again.

Fan

Compressor

Combustion chamber

Turbine

JET POWER

Jet planes have engines called turbofans. A big fan at the front sucks air inside. Some of the air is squashed by a compressor and goes into the combustion chamber. Fuel burned here heats the air. The air expands and rushes out of the engine through a turbine. The spinning turbine drives the fan and compressor.

A jet engine uses the force of hot air to power an aircraft.

FIRST TO FLY

On December 17, 1903, a flimsy aircraft rose into the air near Kitty Hawk in North Carolina, USA, and made the first-ever aeroplane flight.

LEARNING TO FLY

The first aeroplane was called Flyer. It was built by two brothers, Orville and Wilbur Wright. After four years spent building kites and gliders to learn how to steer a plane in the air, they were finally ready to build their first powered aircraft, Flyer.

Wires
Pull the wings tightly against the struts

Struts
Hold the wings the right distance apart

The world's first aeroplane was a biplane – it had two wings, one above the other.

The Wright Flyer

Length	6.4 metres
Wingspan	12.3 metres
Weight	274 kg
Top speed	48 kph (29.8 mph)

The Flyer's engine could only run for a few minutes before it overheated, but that was long enough for the Flyer's short flights.

> The strange-looking 14-bis aircraft was built like big box-kites joined together. Its engine drove a propeller at the back.

Fabric
Covered a wooden frame

Pilot
Sat in a wicker balloon basket

EUROPEAN PLANES

People in Europe were trying to build planes at the same time as the Wright brothers. The first aeroplane flight in Europe was made in France in 1906, by a plane called 14-bis. The first aeroplane flight in Britain was made in 1908. This plane was so big and heavy it was nicknamed 'The Flying Cathedral'!

STEERING

Birds steer in the air by twisting their wings. The wings of the Wright Flyer twisted in the same way. The pilot lay in a cradle which he pulled from side to side. Sliding the cradle to the side pulled wires that pulled the ends of the wings and twisted the wing-tips. They called it wing-warping.

FAST FACTS
First Flight
The Flyer's first flight was about 36 metres long. That's shorter than a Jumbo Jet's passenger cabin!

9

CLASSIC PLANES

Early planes were called stringbags, because they were made of wood and fabric held together with wire. They were soon replaced by all-metal aeroplanes that went faster and faster.

Cockpit
For a crew of three

Engines
Two 900–1,200 horsepower Wright Cyclone piston engines

Propellers
Three metal blades each

Passenger cabin
With 28 seats or 14 beds

THE CLASSIC DC-3

The most popular airliner of the 1930s was the Douglas DC-3. It carried up to 28 people in more comfort than air passengers were used to at that time. The seats were padded and the passenger cabin was heated. A sleeper version had beds for 14 passengers for overnight flights.

> *The DC-3 was the favourite airliner of the 1930s.*

Landing gear
Folded up under wings

Passenger cabin
Room for up to 44 passengers

Engines
Four de Havilland Ghost jets inside the wings

Cockpit
For a crew of four

The de Havilland Comet was the world's first jet airliner in 1952. Its jet engines were buried inside its wings.

Metal skin
Glued to the frame underneath

Wings
All-metal construction

Growing Planes
Concorde grew about 15 centimetres longer during each flight because its metal skin heated up and expanded!

FASTER THAN SOUND

Jet planes went faster and faster until the bullet-shaped Bell X-1 flew faster than sound on October 14, 1947. Supersonic (faster than sound) fighters and bombers were soon built. Then, in 1969, the first supersonic airliner made its first flight. The plane was called Concorde and it carried passengers in comfort at twice the speed of sound.

Concorde was able to fly so fast because of its slim body, dart-shaped wings and four immensely powerful Olympus jet engines.

11

GIANT AIRLINERS

The Boeing 747 'Jumbo Jet' was the biggest airliner in the world for 35 years – it just grew and grew!

FLYING JUMBOS

The Boeing 747 Jumbo Jet made its first flight in 1969 and started carrying passengers the following year. Bigger and bigger Jumbo Jets were then built. The biggest is the 747–400. Each aircraft is built from six million parts. Over the years, Jumbo Jets have flown 3.5 billion passengers a distance of about 56 billion kilometres (34 billion miles) – enough to make 74,000 trips to the Moon and back!

Tail fin
As tall as a six-storey building

A fully loaded 747–400 takes off with about 240,000 litres of fuel and 5 tonnes of food and drink.

Upper deck
Seating for about 205 passengers

The Airbus A380 has the most modern computerised cockpit of any airliner.

The A380 is big enough to have a restaurant, a shop or a cinema.

Main deck
Seating for about 350 passengers

DOUBLE-DECKER

The Airbus A380 is the biggest civil aircraft ever built. Its wheels weigh more than a whole aeroplane of the 1930s. It made its first flight on April 27, 2005. It can carry as many as 840 people on two decks, although airlines will probably put in seats for only 555 passengers.

FAST FACTS
Giant Wings
An aircraft as big as the A380 needs huge wings to lift it. The A380's wings are big enough for more than 70 cars to park on!

	Airbus A380	747-400
Length	73 metres	70.7 metres
Wingspan	79.8 metres	64.4 metres
Maximum take-off weight	560 tonnes	397 tonnes
Passengers	555	416

The double-deck Airbus A380 can carry one-third more people than a Jumbo Jet.

13

BIZJETS

Airline routes and timetables suit most people, but business people sometimes want to go where the big airlines don't land. One answer is the business jet, or bizjet.

SMALL JETS

Bizjets are smaller than airliners, so they can land at thousands of small airports and airfields that bigger airliners can't use. The Learjet is one of the most famous bizjets. Learjets have been flying since the 1960s. They have a crew of two and they can carry up to nine passengers. Other bizjets include the Cessna Citation, Gulfstream, Dassault Falcon and Boeing Business Jet.

Tailplane
At the top of the tail fin

The Learjet is powered by two jet engines behind its wings. It can carry up to nine passengers.

14

Some bizjets are fitted out like offices so that the passengers can work during a flight.

COMPUTER COCKPITS

The latest bizjets have computerised cockpits, just like bigger airliners. The pilots sit in front of computer screens. The plane's computers make it easier to fly and safer, too. Each screen shows all the information that used to be provided by dozens of different dials and gauges in older cockpits.

FAST FACTS
Glass Cockpits
The computerised cockpits used by airliners and bizjets are also called glass cockpits, because of their computer screens. The screens show a wide range of information about the plane and its engines.

This bizjet cockpit has four computer screens full of information for the two pilots.

FLYING FAST

Fast planes dash through the sky at more than 3,000 kph (1,864 mph), three times faster than the speed of sound.

SPEEDY BLACKBIRD

The Lockheed SR-71 Blackbird spy plane is officially the world's fastest plane. It has held the world air speed record since 1976. This plane flies so high that the crew of two wear flight suits like spacesuits. It was designed to fly high and fast to avoid attack from fighters and missiles. It carries no weapons of its own.

The Blackbird has a flattened body and delta (triangle-shaped) wing.

Body
Made from lightweight titanium metal

Engines
Specially designed jet engines

Inlet spike
Moves out or in to let the right amount of air into the engine

Cockpits
Two cockpits, one behind the other

Sensor bays
Contain cameras and other spy equipment

Lockheed SR-71 Blackbird

Length	32.7 metres
Wingspan	16.9 metres
Weight	65,770 kg
Ceiling (most height)	25,900 metres
Top speed	3,529 kph (2,193 mph)

The MiG-25 is also known as the Foxbat. It can fly at 3,000 kph (1,865 mph).

Body
Made of steel and titanium to withstand high temperatures

MIGHTY MIG

The Russian MiG-25 is nearly as fast as the Blackbird. The MiG-25 is a type of fighter called an interceptor. Its job is to fly out to stop enemy planes as fast as possible. It also works as a spy plane when it is loaded with cameras instead of missiles.

Blackbird crews dress like astronauts, because they fly so high.

FAST FACTS
Super-hot Plane

Fast planes like the Blackbird heat up as they fly through the air. At top speed, parts of the Blackbird are five times hotter than boiling water!

17

MEGA FREIGHTERS

The world's biggest aeroplanes are cargo carriers. Some cargo planes are converted airliners. Others are specially designed as freighters.

THE MIGHTY GALAXY

The Lockheed C-5 Galaxy is bigger than a Jumbo Jet. It's big enough to carry 16 army trucks or two 70-tonne battle tanks. Fully loaded, it weighs as much as 40 business jets! When these giant planes are not transporting military equipment, they sometimes carry emergency supplies to the victims of floods and earthquakes.

With its nose raised and ramp lowered, the Galaxy's gigantic cargo hold comes into view.

A giant Galaxy transporter has a crew of seven – two pilots, two flight engineers and three loadmasters.

The C-17 Globemaster's cargo hold can be changed quickly to carry cargo, soldiers or hospital patients on stretchers.

U.S. AIR FORCE

SKY MASTER

The Galaxy is so big that it needs a long runway to land. The C-17 Globemaster is designed to be able to land 77 tonnes of equipment at small airfields. It can even go backwards on the ground to turn round in small spaces.

FAST FACTS
Shuttle Carrier
The Antonov An-225 is the biggest transport plane ever. Only one was built to carry Russia's space shuttle on its back.

U.S. AIR FORCE

9011
439 AW

FIGHTERS

Fighters are aeroplanes designed to attack other planes. Keeping enemy planes at bay is important, because it lets soldiers move about on the ground with more safety.

FEROCIOUS RAPTOR

The F/A-22 Raptor is a new fighter named after a ferocious bird of prey. The 'F/A' in its name means that it can work as a fighter and also as a ground attack plane. It can fly at twice the speed of sound. When it meets an enemy plane, it can turn quickly to fight an air battle.

Jet engines
Two, specially designed for the Raptor

The F/A-22 Raptor carries its weapons inside its body so that they don't spoil its smooth, sleek shape.

Engine nozzles
Swivel for fast turns

Cockpit
For one person

Computers
Link the plane to all nearby Raptors

Big air intakes
Guide lots of air inside to the engines

> The F-15E can work as a fighter or as a bomber. Fighters that also drop bombs are called fighter-bombers.

Fuel tank
Carries extra fuel for long flights

Weapons
Up to 11,000 kg of bombs and missiles

> A fighter cockpit is packed with computers, instruments and controls.

FIGHTING EAGLES

The F/A-22 was designed to replace another great fighter, the F-15 Eagle. The F-15 has ruled the skies since the 1970s. It can fly at over twice the speed of sound. Missiles and bombs hang underneath the plane's body and there is a gun in the nose.

FAST FACTS

Crew Facts

Early F-15s had a crew of one. The latest F-15s have a weapons officer sitting behind the pilot so the pilot can concentrate on flying the plane.

HOVERFLIES

Hoverflies are insects that can stay still in the same spot in mid-air. Some aircraft can do this, too. Most of them are helicopters, but Harrier and Osprey aeroplanes also hover.

TILTING ENGINES

The V-22 Osprey's engines can swivel. When its huge propellers start spinning, it takes off straight upwards like a helicopter. Then the engines and propellers tilt forwards and the plane flies forwards in the normal way. The Osprey is a military transporter. It carries troops or cargo.

3. Flying forwards

2. Engines tilt

1. Take-off

An Osprey swivels its engines after take-off.

JUMP-JET

The Harrier 'Jump-Jet' is a jet plane that can take off straight up in the air. Its secret is a special engine. The jet from the engine comes out through four nozzles – two at the front and two at the back. The pilot can turn the nozzles. When they point down, they push the plane upwards. Then the pilot swivels them backwards to fly forwards. This is called vectored thrust.

FAST FACTS

Jet Steering

The Harrier can't steer in the normal way when it's hovering. Instead, it puffs air from tiny nozzles in its nose, tail and wing-tips.

The Harrier doesn't need a runway – it can land anywhere.

Harrier II

Length	14.6 metres
Wingspan	9.3 metres
Speed	1,065 kph (662 mph)
Weapons	25mm cannon and 6,000 kg of bombs and missiles

MIGHTY AIRCRAFT

INVISIBLE PLANES

Some warplanes are specially designed to be invisible to an enemy. These planes are called stealth planes.

Engines
On top of the wings to hide them from missiles and radar below

Computers
136 computers help the B-2 to fly and complete its mission

Shape
Tested in wind tunnels for 24,000 hours

Cockpit
For a crew of two – the aircraft commander and the mission commander

Weapons
Carried in two bays in the middle of the body

The B-2 bomber is a type of plane called a flying wing. Its body is built from 900 different materials and a million parts.

A B-2 bomber can reach anywhere on Earth by refuelling in the air from a tanker-plane.

PLANE SPOTTING
Stealth planes aren't really invisible, but they don't show up on enemy radar screens like other planes. Most planes appear as glowing spots on a radar screen. Stealth planes don't appear on radar because of their strange shape. The B-2 bomber is a stealth plane.

The Nighthawk's computers are programmed with its mission and then it flies automatically to its target.

NIGHTHAWK

The F-117 Nighthawk was built before the B-2 to prove that stealth planes really can hide from enemy radar. The hot gases from its two engines leave the plane through a wide slot at the back. This cools the gases quickly so that heat-seeking missiles find it hard to hit the plane.

FAST FACTS
The Power of the B-2
Each B-2 can carry out a bombing raid that used to need 75 older bombers, fighters and other support planes.

Military pilots sit in ejection seats. If the plane is going to crash, a rocket blasts the seat clear of the plane.

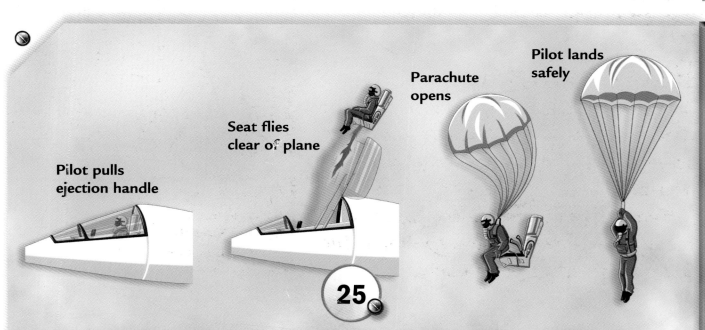

Pilot pulls ejection handle

Seat flies clear of plane

Parachute opens

Pilot lands safely

SPECIALS

Most planes are made in large numbers, but some planes are unique – only one is built. These special planes are built for a special flight or to set a new record.

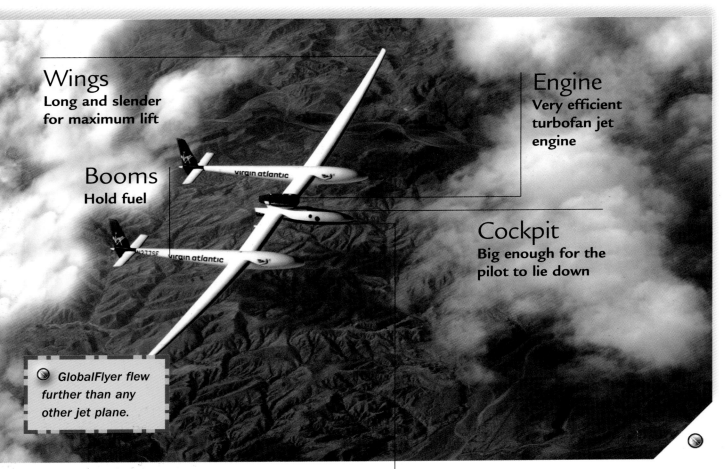

Wings
Long and slender for maximum lift

Booms
Hold fuel

Engine
Very efficient turbofan jet engine

Cockpit
Big enough for the pilot to lie down

GlobalFlyer flew further than any other jet plane.

Centre pod
Contains cockpit

ROUND THE WORLD

On March 1, 2005, Steve Fossett climbed into a plane called GlobalFlyer and took off. Two days later, he landed at the same airfield in Kansas, USA. He had become the first person to fly around the world non-stop on his own. Two pilots had made the first non-stop round-the-world flight 19 years earlier in a plane called Voyager.

Wings
Made from strong lightweight carbon fibre

Propellers
One at the front and one at the back

WHITE KNIGHT

Spaceship One soared into space on June 21, 2004, and made the first private spaceflight. The spacecraft was carried aloft by a strange-looking plane called White Knight. White Knight takes off with the spacecraft slung underneath it. It climbs to a height of 15,250 metres and launches the spacecraft.

FAST FACTS
Perfect Plane

GlobalFlyer was such a perfect shape for flying that the only way to get it to land was to drag parachutes behind it.

White Knight's strange shape lets it carry a spacecraft underneath.

FUTURE PLANES

Plane–makers are always thinking about what future aircraft might look like. Some of their ideas might surprise you.

FUTURE AIRLINERS

The Airbus A380 is the biggest airliner today, but future airliners might be even bigger. One future design for an airliner looks like a B-2 bomber, but with seats for 1,000 passengers inside its wings. Rocket-powered airliners looking like space shuttles could carry passengers around the world at five or ten times the speed of sound.

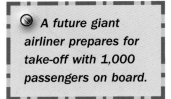

A future giant airliner prepares for take-off with 1,000 passengers on board.

Cabins
For passengers inside the wings

The Global Hawk spy plane is about the same size as a business jet, but it doesn't need a pilot.

ROBOT PLANES

Did you know that aeroplanes don't need pilots? Planes without pilots are called Unmanned Air Vehicles, or UAVs. The simplest UAVs are flown by a pilot sitting in a cockpit on the ground. Moving the controls sends radio signals to the plane to steer it. Smarter UAVs fly themselves. A spy plane called Global Hawk is one of these smart UAVs. It is flown by its own computers.

FAST FACTS
Spy Flight
In April 2001, a pilotless Global Hawk spy plane flew itself all the way across the Pacific Ocean from the USA to Australia.

Engine
Small jet engine inside body

Wings
Wingspan 10.3 metres

The X-45 is an experimental UCAV (Unmanned Combat Air Vehicle) flown by a pilot on the ground. With no pilot inside, it is smaller, faster and turns more tightly than a normal fighter.

29

TIMELINE

1903
The Wright brothers build the first successful aeroplane, the Flyer, and make the first-ever powered flight.

1909
Louis Bleriot makes the first flight across the English Channel in his Bleriot X1 plane.

1919
John Alcock and Arthur Whitten Brown make the first non-stop flight across the Atlantic Ocean in a Vickers Vimy bomber.

1927
Charles Lindbergh makes the first solo non-stop flight across the Atlantic Ocean in his Ryan plane called Spirit of St Louis.

1930
Frank Whittle invents the jet engine.

1947
Charles 'Chuck' Yeager makes the first supersonic (faster than sound) flight in the experimental Bell X-1 rocket plane.

1952
The de Havilland Comet becomes the world's first jet airliner.

1969
The supersonic airliner Concorde makes its first flight.

1969
The Boeing 747 Jumbo Jet makes its first flight.

1976
The Lockheed SR-71 Blackbird spy-plane sets a new world air speed record of 3,529 kph.

1976
The supersonic airliner Concorde begins flying passengers for British Airways and Air France.

1986
Dick Rutan and Jeanna Yeager make the first non-stop round-the-world aeroplane flight in their Voyager plane.

1989
The Northrop B-2 Spirit stealth bomber and V-22 Osprey make their first flights.

1994
The Boeing 777 is the first airliner to be designed using 3-D computer graphics.

1997
The F/A-22 Raptor makes its first flight.

2001
A Global Hawk unmanned spy plane flies across the Pacific Ocean from the USA to Australia.

2004
The White Knight plane launches Spaceship One on the first privately funded spaceflight.

2005
The giant Airbus A380 airliner makes its first flight.

2005
Steve Fossett makes the first solo non-stop round the world aeroplane flight in the GlobalFlyer plane.

GLOSSARY

ailerons
Strips at the back of a plane's wings that swivel up or down to make the plane roll and turn.

bizjet
Another name for a business jet, a small jet plane used as an air taxi for carrying small numbers of people.

cockpit
The part of a plane where the pilot sits. It has the controls for flying the plane and instruments for showing information about the plane.

elevators
Parts of a plane's tail that swivel up or down to make a climb or dive.

fuel
A liquid burned in an aircraft's engine to provide the energy to move the plane.

glider
A plane with no engine. It is towed up into the air and then glides back to the ground. Also called a sail-plane.

horsepower
A unit for measuring the power of an aircraft engine.

missiles
Rocket-powered weapons carried by aircraft. When a missile is launched, it flies towards its target and explodes.

prop-rotors
Parts of a plane with tilting engines that work like helicopter rotors some of the time and propellers the rest of the time.

radar
Equipment for finding a plane by bouncing radio waves off it.

rudder
Part of a plane's tail that swivels to turn the plane's nose to point in a different direction.

stealth plane
A plane designed to be hard to find by radar.

stringbag
A nickname for the type of plane used in the early 1900s, made from wood, fabric and wires.

supersonic
Faster than the speed of sound.

titanium
A strong, lightweight metal used to make the fastest planes, because it can withstand very high temperatures.

UAV
Unmanned Air Vehicle. A plane without a pilot inside. Most UAVs are flown by pilots on the ground, but the latest UAVs are flown by their own computers.

UCAV
Unmanned Combat Air Vehicle. A warplane with no pilot inside.

vectored thrust
A way to steer a plane or make it take off straight up in the air by swivelling the engine nozzles to point in different directions.

wing-warping
A way to steer a plane used by the Wright brothers. It worked by twisting the plane's wing-tips in opposite directions.

INDEX

WEBFINDER

http://www.boeing.com/companyoffices/aboutus/wonder_of_flight/index.html *Find out how things fly*

http://www.boeing.com/companyoffices/aboutus/wonder_of_flight/engine.html *Learn how jet engines work*

http://www.first-to-fly.com *Find out all about the Wright brothers and their aircraft*

http://www.boeing.com/commercial/747family/pf/pf_facts.html *Lots of Jumbo Jet facts*

http://www.sprucegoose.org *Visit this website to find out about the Spruce Goose aircraft*

http://www.virginatlanticglobalflyer.com *The story of the plane that flew non-stop all the way around the world*

http://science.howstuffworks.com/f-22-raptor.htm *Read about the F/A-22 Raptor fighter plane*

http://www.guinnessworldrecords.com *Use this website to find out about record-breaking aircraft*